MICROHABITATS

Life in a
TREE

Clare Oliver

Evans

Evans Brothers Limited

First published in Great Britain in 2002 by Evans Brothers Limited
2A Portman Mansions
Chiltern Street
London W1U 6NR

Project Editors: Sean Dolan, Tamsin Osler, Louise John
Consultant: Michael Chinery
Production Director: Richard Johnson
Illustrated by Stuart Lafford
Designed by Ian Winton

Planned and produced by Discovery Books

British Library Cataloguing in Publication Data
Oliver, Clare
    Life in a tree - (Microhabitats)
    1. Forest animals - Juvenile literature
    I. Title
    578.7'3
    ISBN 0 237 522985

Printed in the United States

Contents

The Oak Tree

Life in a Tree

Every tree is an amazing **microhabitat** – an almost self-contained small environment. This book looks at the many different types of plants and animals that live in, or near, the oak tree. Oaks are broad-leaved trees that grow naturally throughout North America, Europe, and Asia, as well as northern parts of South America and North Africa.

Wasp

There are over 500 different kinds of oak. Most oaks are huge trees that can live for hundreds of years. They can grow as tall as an eight-storey building and the trunks of fully-grown oaks are too wide to stretch your arms around. Some have a circumference of more than 9 metres! Oaks need sunlight to grow and do not do well in the shade.

Bark beetle

Grey squirrel

Barn owl

Vapourer moth caterpillar

Rabbit

Guess What?

Druids (a class of priests, teachers, and judges among the Celts) treated oak trees as temples, and worshipped at them.

The ancient Greeks and Romans regarded oak wood as a symbol of bravery. Their mythical hero Hercules was often shown holding a club made of oak.

In Greek and Roman mythology, dryads were godlike female nymphs or spirits that lived in oak trees.

Many different kinds of birds perch on the branches of the oak tree. Squirrels and other mammals scurry along the branches or nest in the leaf litter. The thick, gnarled trunk supports fungi, ivy and thousands of insects and spiders.

From Little Acorns...

The oak tree starts life as a little acorn, which is the fruit or nut of the adult oak tree. In autumn the acorns drop to the ground, where some of them are eaten by animals and birds. Others are collected and buried by squirrels and jays, as a store of food for the bleak winter months. But sometimes these animals forget to come back for the acorns and this gives them a good start in life. The animals bury the acorns at the right depth in the soil, and as long as they are away from the shadow of the adult tree, they begin to grow on their own.

A tree trunk grows wider each year and a new ring of wood appears underneath the bark. You can tell how old a tree is by counting these rings.

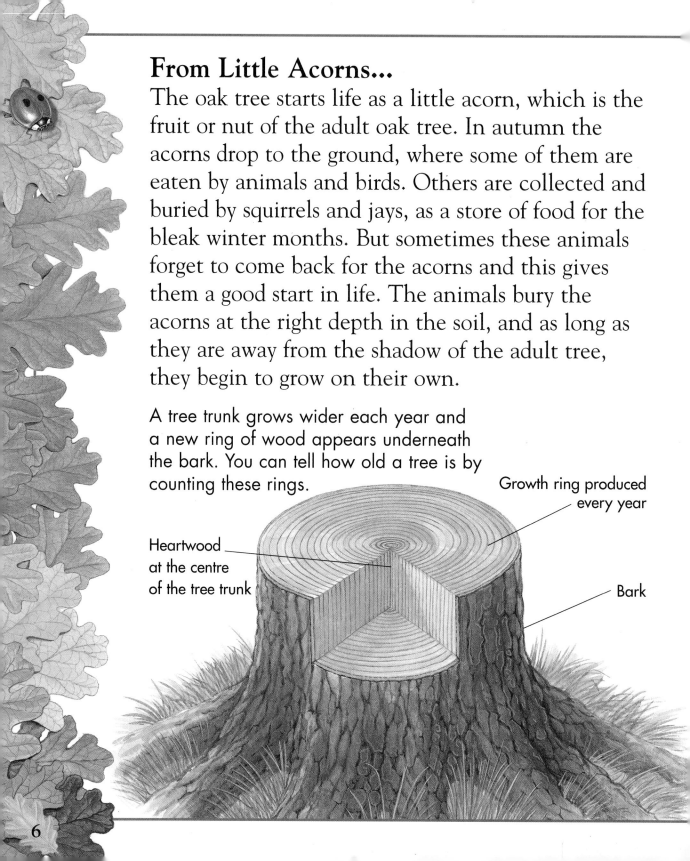

Growth ring produced every year

Heartwood at the centre of the tree trunk

Bark

Life Begins

In **temperate** climates during the spring, the earth is warmed up by the Sun and watered by rain. The warmth and moisture help the acorn to **germinate**. It grows a tiny shoot which eventually becomes the trunk of the tree, and then this divides to make leafy branches.

It is hard to believe that this seedling could grow into an oak tree up to 27m tall.

Guess What?

Oak trees don't produce acorns until they are at least 40 years old.

Native Americans used to eat acorns. Sweeter varieties were eaten like nuts, while bitter ones were ground to make flour for bread.

The acorn also grows a root. This becomes an underground network of roots that supports the tree and sucks up water and nutrients from the soil.

Spring and Summer

Most oaks are deciduous. This means that they grow new leaves every spring. The tree bursts into life and its branches sprout hundreds of buds that open up into shiny green leaves. In the autumn, the tree sheds the leaves and the branches are bare.

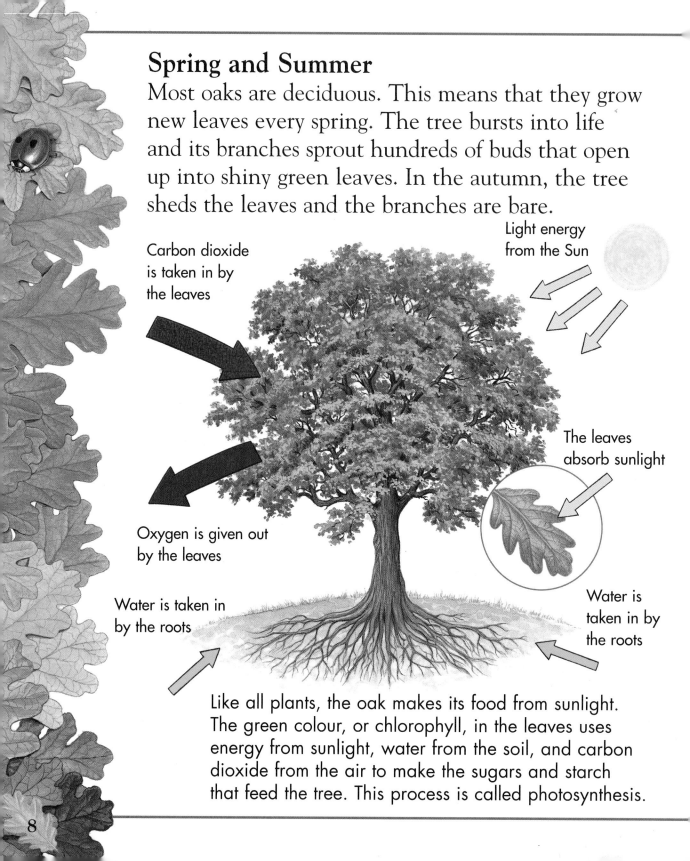

Light energy from the Sun

Carbon dioxide is taken in by the leaves

The leaves absorb sunlight

Oxygen is given out by the leaves

Water is taken in by the roots

Water is taken in by the roots

Like all plants, the oak makes its food from sunlight. The green colour, or chlorophyll, in the leaves uses energy from sunlight, water from the soil, and carbon dioxide from the air to make the sugars and starch that feed the tree. This process is called photosynthesis.

Blowing in the Wind

Oak trees also produce flowers. The buds appear in the spring and flower throughout the summer. Each oak tree grows two types of flowers, or catkins – male and female. The wind blows the tiny grains of pollen from the male flower onto the female flowers and the female flowers are **fertilised**. An acorn then grows from each fertilised female flower. The overlapping scales at the base of the flower become the little cup that holds the acorn.

The male flowers are usually scraggly catkins that dangle from the tree. The tiny female flowers grow singly or in spiky clusters at the tips of the twigs.

See For Yourself

Each kind of oak tree has a slightly different leaf shape. Some have stalks and some don't. Some have jagged **lobes** and some have smooth. See how many different types you can find!

9

Autumn and Winter

In autumn, the deciduous oak tree gets ready for the winter and starts to shed its leaves. Before this happens, the precious green **pigment**, called chlorophyll, which helps the tree make food is broken down. All the useful bits of the chlorophyll are sucked back into the twigs and branches. They are used again the following year by the new leaves.

Without the green pigment, the leaves turn orange, red, yellow and even purple. Finally, they dry out, turn brown and fall to the ground.

An oak tree may lose as many as 250,000 leaves every autumn.

The dead leaves are blown down to the ground. There they rot to make rich leaf litter, which returns the **nutrients** to the soil. By now, ripe acorns have fallen to the ground. Those that are not eaten by hungry animals will spend the winter in a **dormant,** or sleeplike, state.

In winter the ground under an oak tree is covered with dead leaves, acorns and broken twigs.

By the middle of winter, the oak's branches are bare, but its thick bark protects the tree from the cold.

Animal Life

Mammals

Mammals are warm-blooded animals. They feed their babies on the mother's milk and are covered in soft fur or hair. Lots of different mammals live in, or near, the shelter of oak trees.

Bats roost in hollows in the trunks of old oak trees. They come out at night to hunt for insects.

Food and Shelter

Oak trees provide food and shelter for many animals. Mice, squirrels and deer eat the tree's young shoots in the spring and its juicy acorns in the autumn.

Mice and voles make their nests amongst the tree's roots. For warmth, they line the nests with fur and fallen leaves.

A grey squirrel makes a meal of a juicy acorn.

Walls and Ceilings

The tree's thick roots make natural walls and ceilings for the mice and voles that make their nests in them. Bigger mammals, such as rabbits, badgers and foxes make their warrens, sets and dens here, too. Hedgehogs sleep all through the winter in the dead leaves at the bottom of hollow trees. This long winter sleep is called **hibernation**.

Guess What?

Squirrels live in tree hollows or build nests called dreys out of oak leaves and twigs.

The badger has such powerful front paws it can easily outdig a man using a spade.

A red fox pads through the snow in search of food.

Birds

Many different types of bird, including the woodpecker and magpie, make their nests in the oak tree. The birds get a home, but this helps the tree too, because bird droppings are an extra source of nutrients. They help to fertilise, or feed, the tree.

Like bats, barn owls often roost in oak trees during the day.

Visitors to the Oak

Some birds only visit the oak for a rest or a meal. Acorns provide food for crows, rooks, jays, and wood pigeons. Wood pigeons can eat as many as 120 acorns in a day! Crows, rooks, and jays eat insects that live in the tree, too. They also prey on other, smaller birds.

Songbirds such as warblers and wrens stop to gulp down a juicy caterpillar or two. Many other birds, such as the robin and the song thrush, also perch high in the oak's branches, singing to attract a mate.

Wrens like to make their nests in small holes in the trunks of oak trees.

See For Yourself

If you spot acorns or hazelnuts wedged into the bark of an oak tree, that's a sign that nuthatches have been busy storing food for the winter. The birds return and eat the food later!

If you find a neat little pellet of bones and feathers or fur under an oak tree, you can be sure that an owl has been in the tree. Owls swallow their prey whole, then cough up a pellet.

This feather belongs to a pheasant. You can tell because it is long and colourful with banded markings along its length.

15

Crawling Insects

As many as 500 species of insect depend on the oak tree for food. Underground, the **larvae**, or grubs, of click beetles munch through the tree's roots. Above ground, in the leaf litter at the base of the tree, earwigs can usually be found looking for food.

Bark, Branches and Leaves

Bark lice climb over the oak tree's bark whilst bark beetle grubs gnaw into the wood beneath. The leaves are munched by other hungry beetles.
In autumn, weevils drill into the acorns with their long snouts to get at the sweet kernel inside.

When the acorn weevil drills into an acorn, it eats some of the sweet kernel before laying its eggs inside.

Insect Eggs

Some weevils lay their eggs inside acorns, while many gall wasps lay their eggs in the tree's buds. Where this happens, the oak produces a gall – a kind of swollen scab, with the gall wasp grubs inside it.

Oak apple galls are caused by a tiny gall wasp. A large oak apple might contain up to 30 wasp grubs.

See For Yourself

Look out for these orange spots on the underside of oak leaves. These are called spangle galls, and inside each one is the tiny grub of a gall wasp.

Look for holes in an oak apple gall. This is where fully grown gall wasps have emerged.

Butterflies and Moths

Butterflies and moths often lay their eggs on the leaves of the oak tree. That way, when the caterpillars hatch, they have lots of juicy leaves to eat! Big caterpillars munch right through the leaves, but some caterpillars are so small that they make tiny tunnels between the top and bottom surfaces of the leaves.

Moth caterpillars can strip an oak tree of its leaves.

Tortoiseshell butterflies often hibernate through the winter in hollow trees.

These mottled umber moths are well camouflaged among dead oak leaves.

Guess What?

Can you guess what carpenter moth caterpillars eat? The name gives you a clue: wood.

Sometimes oaks lose so many leaves to hungry caterpillars that they have to sprout a second set of leaves.

Micromoths are tiny. Some have a wingspan of under 5mm. It is easy for them to hide in small cracks in the oak's bark.

Woodland Wings

Woodland moths are usually coloured to blend in with their surroundings. This makes it hard for birds and other enemies to see them. Moths that rest on leaves are usually some shade of green. Those that rest on tree trunks are usually some shade of brown.

Web of Life

Hunters and Their Prey

Juicy caterpillars and greenfly that feed on the oak tree attract hunters that feed on them! The hunters include wasps, ladybirds, spiders and birds.

Orb-web spiders mainly feed on insects that they catch in the sticky threads of their webs.

A blue tit feeding a hungry brood might collect several hundred caterpillars in a day. However, its eggs or even its chicks might end up in the stomach of a larger bird, such as a magpie, jay or owl.

Guess What?

Most ladybirds are red, but some are bright yellow, orange or black.

Tree creepers climb up the trunk in a spiral!

Cuckoos do not bother feeding their own chicks. They lay their eggs in another bird's nest and make them do all the work!

Feeding on Grubs

Other birds come to feast on the grubs under the bark. Spotted woodpeckers and tree creepers have strong feet for clinging to the trunk and specially shaped beaks for dragging the grubs out.

Woodpeckers also have very long tongues, which they push into holes to search for insect grubs.

21

Plant Life

Ferns and mosses are moisture-loving plants that grow well in the shade of the oak tree. Mushrooms and toadstools also grow here, usually appearing in the autumn. They cannot make their own food like green plants, so they break down the oak's dead leaves and twigs and feed on these. Nutrients from the dead leaves are also taken up by the tree roots and used for new growth.

Even an old, dead oak tree is a microhabitat. Mites and beetles like this stag beetle feed on the dead wood, while fungi takes over the bark.

Climbing High

Not all plants are useful to the oak. Ivy scrambles up the oak's trunk towards the light, clinging with little suckers called rootlets. As the ivy spreads, it covers the tree's own leaves.

Ivy climbing up the trunk of this oak tree covers the leaves and blocks out the sunlight.

This prevents the oak from getting enough light to make food, which can weaken it so much that it can die.

Mistletoe is a parasite that causes harm by pushing roots through the oak's bark to steal nutrients from it.

Other Trees

Broad-Leaved Trees

Oaks belong to the group of trees called broad-leaved trees: their leaves are broad and flat. Other broad-leaved trees include beeches, maples and fruit trees. Most of these are deciduous trees, which means they lose their leaves in winter. They blossom in spring and produce seeds in autumn. However, over 200 kinds of oak are evergreens, meaning that they keep their leaves through all the seasons.

Many types of cherry tree are grown for their blossoms as well as their fruit. Japanese cherry trees like this one are grown because their flowers are so beautiful.

Insect Attractors

Cherry, horse chestnut and apple trees have much more colourful flowers than the oak. This is because they need to attract insects to **pollinate** their flowers. The oak tree is pollinated by the wind.

The colour and smell of an apple blossom attracts a bee.

Going to Seed

In autumn, the fruits of broad-leaved trees attract many kinds of birds. The birds get a meal, but they, in turn, help the tree. The seeds inside the fruit pass through the birds and come out in their droppings. In time, new trees may grow from these seeds.

Sweet chestnuts are enclosed in spiny cases to stop animals and birds from eating them.

Other Types of Tree

Not all trees are deciduous like the oak. Trees that keep their leaves throughout the year are called evergreens. Conifers are evergreen trees that grow cones. They also have tough needles, which survive both heat and cold. Their branches slope and the snow slips right off them. Birds that eat their seeds include the crossbill. It pokes the seeds out of the cone with its specially shaped beak.

The pine tree in the above picture is a type of conifer. The needles have a waxy coating that stops them from losing water and drying out.

The pine marten hunts in the branches of pine trees. It eats birds, their eggs and also insects.

Tropical Trees

In the tropics, where there is no cold winter, most trees keep their leaves all year. These trees include palms that grow coconuts and dates, and tropical fruit trees that grow fruit such as mangoes and paw paws.

The delicious nuts and fruits of tropical trees attract monkeys and birds.

Guess What?

Bristlecone pines, which grow in the Rocky Mountains in North America, live longer than any other type of conifer. One bristlecone in Nevada, USA, is about 4,900 years old.

The tropical coco-de-mer tree, which grows on the Seychelles Islands in the Indian Ocean, produces the biggest fruit of any plant. Its nuts weigh as much as 20 kg and can take 10 years to ripen fully.

A lemur can gorge on as many as 500 figs a week!

The Importance of Trees

Save the Trees!

Like the oak, all trees provide animals and plants with precious food or shelter. Some animals even depend on one particular type of tree for their survival. Koalas, for example, will only feed on the leaves of the eucalyptus tree.

Trees and Us

Trees are beautiful to look at but they are very important to us, too. Photosynthesis provides much of the oxygen that humans and other animals need to breathe. Many trees produce edible fruits and nuts, such as hazelnuts and apples. They also provide us with wood, one of our most useful natural materials.

Sometimes people hurry to clear away fallen trees, branches, and logs from the forest floor. However, even fallen and dead trees can be a habitat for insects and small mammals, as well as for other plant life.

What We Can Do

We must make sure there are trees for people to enjoy in the future. We must not chop down more than we plant. We must also stop or reduce pollution wherever possible, because it damages trees and the environment on which trees depend for their health.

Guess What?

About 87 per cent of the original rain forests of North America have been cut down. A further 7 per cent is likely to be felled. The remaining forest may not be large enough to support the wildlife that lives there now.

Only 6 per cent of the world's tropical forests are protected by law. The rest is threatened by commercial tree felling.

In the 20th century, a fungus called Dutch elm disease destroyed millions of trees in Europe and America.

Two lumberjacks felling trees in a forest for commercial use.

Glossary

Dormant: Not active. An acorn is dormant during the winter, when it is too cold to grow.

Fertilise: To make something able to produce fruit, seeds, or offspring.

Germinate: To make something sprout and develop.

Hibernation: A sleeplike state in which some animals exist during the coldest months of the year.

Larva: An insect baby, such as a beetle grub, that looks nothing like its parent.

Lobe: The parts of the edge of an oak leaf that stick out.

Microhabitat: A small, specialised place, such as a tree, pond, or rock pool, where particular plants and animals live.

Nutrient: A substance that nourishes (feeds) a plant or animal, for example any of the minerals found in soil.

Pigment: A chemical that gives colouring to something. Chlorophyll is the pigment that makes leaves look green.

Pollinate: To transfer male pollen to female flower parts. Plants might rely on wind, insects, birds or other animals to move the pollen.

Temperate: A climate that varies with the seasons and is not characterised by either the extreme cold of the polar regions or the high temperatures and humidity of the tropics.

Index

Acknowledgements

The publishers would like to thank the following for permission to reproduce their pictures:

Front cover: Kim Taylor/Bruce Coleman Collection; p.7: P. Kaya/Oxford Scientific Films; p.9: Gordon Maclean/Oxford Scientific Films; p.10: N.A. Callow/Natural History Photographic Agency; p.11t: Chris Fairclough/Discovery Picture Library; p.11b: Tim Shepherd/Oxford Scientific Films; p.12t: Stephen Dalton/Natural History Photographic Agency; p.12b: Jane Burton/Bruce Coleman Collection; p.13: PhotoLink/PhotoDisc; p.14: Hans Reinhard/Bruce Coleman Collection; p.15: Richard Day/Oxford Scientific Films; p.16: David Wright/Oxford Scientific Films; p.17: Andrew Purcell/Bruce Coleman Collection; p.18: Kim Taylor/Bruce Coleman Collection; p.19: Kim Taylor/Bruce Coleman Collection; p.20: Jane Burton/Bruce Coleman Collection; p.21: Hans Reinhard/Bruce Coleman Collection; p.22: G.I.Bernard/Oxford Scientific Films; p.23: Chris Fairclough Picture Library; p.24: PhotoLink/PhotoDisc; p.25t: PhotoLink/Photodisc; p.25b: Chris Fairclough Picture Library; p.26t: Dr Eckart Pott/Bruce Coleman Collection; p.26b: William S. Paton/Bruce Coleman Collection; p.27: PhotoLink/PhotoDisc; p.28: Terry Heathcote/Oxford Scientific Films; p.29: Malcolm Penny.